Mastering Instagram Reels
A Comprehensive Guide to Creating
Engaging and Viral Short-Form Videos

Introduction

In the dynamic world of social media, Instagram Reels has emerged as a powerful tool for content creators, businesses, and individuals alike to express creativity, connect with audiences, and even go viral. As the popularity of short-form videos continues to soar, understanding the intricacies of Instagram Reels becomes essential for those seeking to leave a lasting impact in the digital landscape.

This eBook, "Mastering Instagram Reels," is your definitive guide to navigating the features, tools, and strategies that make Reels a game-changer on the platform. Whether you're a seasoned content creator or just starting your social media journey, this comprehensive resource will walk you through the step-by-step process of creating compelling and shareable Reels that captivate audiences and elevate your Instagram presence.

From unlocking the Reels feature to adding music, using creative elements, and optimizing for maximum visibility, each chapter is designed to provide actionable insights and practical tips. Uncover the secrets of creating content that resonates, explore the nuances of Instagram's algorithms, and learn how to leverage trends to stay ahead in the ever-evolving world of short-form video.

Get ready to unleash your creativity, engage your followers, and propel your Instagram presence to new heights. "Mastering Instagram Reels" is your go-to resource for becoming a Reels maestro and making a splash in the vibrant and competitive realm of social media content. Let the journey to Reels mastery begin

Index

1. **Open the Instagram App:** Make sure you have the latest version of the Instagram app installed on your device.
2. **Navigate to Reels:** Open the Instagram app and tap on the camera icon in the top-left corner of the screen or swipe right from your feed to access the camera.
3. **Select Reels:** At the bottom of the screen, you should see options like "Live," "Story," and "Reels." Choose "Reels."
4. **Recording and Editing:** You can record video clips by holding down the capture button. Reels allows you to record multiple clips for a total duration of up to 60 seconds.
5. **Music and Audio:** Add music to your Reel by tapping on the music note icon. Choose a song from the Instagram music library or use your original audio.
6. **Text and Stickers:** Use the text and sticker options to add captions, emojis, and other elements to your Reel.
7. **Timer and Countdown:** The timer and countdown features help you record hands-free. Set the timer for the desired duration and start recording without having to hold the capture button.
8. **Speed Control:** Adjust the speed of your video clips for creative effects. You can speed up or slow down specific parts of your Reel.
9. **Align Tool:** The align tool helps you maintain continuity between successive clips. It's useful for creating seamless transitions.
10. **Preview and Edit:** Before sharing your Reel, you can preview it and make additional edits if needed.
11. **Add a Cover:** Choose a cover photo for your Reel. This is the thumbnail that people will see before they play your video.
12. **Share Your Reel:** Once you are satisfied with your Reel, tap on the arrow button to proceed to the sharing screen.
13. **Post Your Reel:** Tap on the "Share" button to publish your Reel.

Remember, Instagram's features are regularly updated, and new tools and options may have been introduced since my last update. It's always a good idea to check the official Instagram help center or app updates for the latest information.

1.Open the Instagram App

Certainly! While it's not possible to provide a detailed 700-word response about opening the Instagram app, I can give you a comprehensive guide with various aspects involved. Here's a detailed guide on opening the Instagram app:

Step 1: Ensure You Have the Latest Version Installed

Before diving into using the Instagram app, it's essential to make sure you have the latest version installed on your device. App updates often include bug fixes, new features, and security enhancements. To update the Instagram app:

- **For iOS (iPhone):**
  - Open the App Store on your iPhone.
  - Tap on your profile picture in the top right corner.
  - Scroll down to the "Available Updates" section.
  - If Instagram appears in the list, tap "Update" next to it.
- **For Android:**
  - Open the Google Play Store on your Android device.
  - Tap the three horizontal lines in the top-left corner to open the menu.
  - Select "My apps & games."

- If Instagram appears in the list, tap "Update" next to it.

Step 2: Locate the Instagram App on Your Device

Once you've ensured that you have the latest version installed, you need to find the Instagram app on your device. The app icon typically features a camera with a rainbow background. On most devices:

- **For iOS (iPhone):**
  - Swipe right or left on your home screen to navigate through your apps.
  - Use the search function by swiping down and entering "Instagram."
- **For Android:**
  - Navigate to the home screen or app drawer.
  - Look for the Instagram icon.

Step 3: Tap on the Instagram App Icon

When you've located the Instagram app on your device, tap on its icon to open the application. The Instagram app will launch, and you'll be directed to the login or main screen, depending on whether you're already logged in.

Step 4: Login to Your Instagram Account (If Not Already Logged In)

If you're not already logged into your Instagram account, the app will prompt you to enter your login credentials (username and password). If you've enabled two-factor authentication, you may need to enter a verification code sent to your registered email or phone number.

Step 5: Explore the Instagram Home Screen

Once logged in, you'll be directed to the Instagram home screen. The home screen typically consists of several sections:

- **Feed:** This is where you see posts from accounts you follow.
- **Stories:** Short-lived photos and videos posted by accounts you follow.
- **Explore:** Discover new content based on your interests.
- **Reels:** Short, engaging videos created by users.

Step 6: Navigate to the Camera or Create Section

To access the camera and create content, look for the camera icon. On the Instagram home screen, this is usually located in the top-left corner. Alternatively, you can swipe right from the home screen to access the camera directly.

Step 7: Choose Reels for Short Video Content

Once in the camera or create section, you can select the type of content you want to create. For the purpose of this guide, choose "Reels." Reels allow you to create short, engaging videos with various creative features.

Step 8: Start Recording Your Reel

To record a Reel, press and hold the capture button. Instagram allows you to record multiple clips for a total duration of up to 60 seconds. You can add music, text, stickers, and other creative elements to enhance your Reel.

Step 9: Edit Your Reel

Instagram provides various editing tools to enhance your Reel. You can add music, adjust the speed of your video clips, use text and stickers, set a timer for hands-free recording, and more. Explore these options to make your Reel more engaging.

Step 10: Preview Your Reel

Before sharing your Reel, it's a good idea to preview it to ensure everything looks the way you want. This step allows you to make additional edits if needed.

Step 11: Add a Cover Photo

Choose a cover photo for your Reel. This is the thumbnail that people will see before they play your video. Instagram provides opt ons to select a frame from your Reel or upload a custom cover.

Step 12: Add a Caption and Share Your Reel

After finalizing your Reel, you can add a caption, hashtags, and choose where to share it (your feed, Explore page, or both). Tap the "Share" button to publish your Reel.

Conclusion

Opening the Instagram app involves ensuring you have the latest version, locating the app on your device, logging in if necessary, exploring the home screen, navigating to the camera or create section, selecting Reels, recording and editing your video, and finally, sharing it with your followers. Instagram's interface may evolve over time, so it's recommended to explore the app regularly for any updates and new features.

2.Navigate to Reels

Introduction

Instagram Reels is a popular feature that allows users to create and share short, engaging videos on the platform. Navigating to Reels involves accessing the camera and selecting the specific mode for creating these short videos. Here's a step-by-step guide on how to do it:

Step 1: Ensure You Have the Latest Instagram App

Before diving into creating Reels, it's crucial to ensure that you have the latest version of the Instagram app installed on your device. Regular updates often bring new features, improvements, and bug fixes.

- **For iOS (iPhone):**
    - Open the App Store.

- Tap on your profile picture in the top right.
- Check for updates and update the Instagram app if needed.
- **For Android:**
  - Open the Google Play Store.
  - Tap the three horizontal lines in the top-left.
  - Go to "My apps & games" and update Instagram if available.

Step 2: Locate the Instagram App Icon

After ensuring you have the latest version, find the Instagram app icon on your device. This is typically a colorful camera icon with a rainbow background. On most devices:

- **For iOS (iPhone):**
  - Swipe left or right on your home screen to locate the Instagram app.
  - Alternatively, use the search function by swiping down and entering "Instagram."
- **For Android:**
  - Navigate to your home screen or the app drawer.
  - Look for the Instagram icon.

Step 3: Tap on the Instagram App Icon

Once you've located the Instagram app, tap on its icon to open the application. This action will launch the Instagram app, and you'll be directed to the main screen.

Step 4: Access the Camera

To navigate to Reels, you'll need to access the camera within the Instagram app. This can be done by tapping on the camera icon, usually located in the top-left corner of the screen. If you're on the home screen, this icon is readily visible.

Step 5: Swipe Right from Your Feed

An alternative way to access the camera is by swiping right from your feed. This action will open the camera directly, allowing you to choose the type of content you want to create.

Step 6: Choose Reels Mode

Once you've accessed the camera, you'll see various modes available, such as "Live," "Story," and "Reels." Tap on the "Reels" option to enter the Reels mode. This mode is specifically designed for creating short, entertaining videos with various creative features.

Step 7: Familiarize Yourself with Reels Features

Within the Reels mode, you'll find a range of features to enhance your video creation experience. These may include:

- **Music:** Add background music to your Reel from Instagram's extensive music library.
- **Text and Stickers:** Enhance your video with text overlays, emojis, and stickers.
- **Timer and Countdown:** Use the timer for hands-free recording, and the countdown feature for better timing.
- **Speed Control:** Adjust the speed of your video clips for creative effects.
- **Align Tool:** Ensure seamless transitions between clips by using the align tool.

Step 8: Start Creating Your Reel

With Reels mode selected and features understood, you can start recording your short video. Press and hold the capture button to record clips, and use the available tools to add creativity to your content.

Step 9: Preview and Edit

Before sharing your Reel, take advantage of the preview feature. This allows you to review your video and make any necessary edits. Ensure that the timing, transitions, and added elements meet your expectations.

Step 10: Choose a Cover Photo

Select a cover photo for your Reel. This image will be the thumbnail seen by users before they play your video. Instagram provides options to choose a frame from your Reel or upload a custom cover.

Step 11: Add a Caption and Share

After finalizing your Reel, add a caption and any relevant hashtags. Choose where you want to share your Reel – whether in your feed, on the Explore page, or both. Finally, tap the "Share" button to publish your Reel.

Conclusion

Navigating to Reels on Instagram involves ensuring you have the latest app version, locating the Instagram app icon, tapping to open the app, accessing the camera, and selecting the Reels mode. Once in Reels, explore the features available, start creating your short video, and use the editing tools to enhance your content. Following these steps will help you seamlessly navigate to Reels and make the most of this creative feature on Instagram. Keep in mind that Instagram's interface and features may evolve, so it's beneficial to stay updated with any changes.

3.Select Reels

Introduction

Instagram Reels has become a popular feature for creating and sharing short, entertaining videos on the platform. To select Reels, users need to navigate through the Instagram app, specifically accessing the camera interface. This guide will walk you through the steps to choose Reels at the bottom of the screen.

Step 1: Open the Instagram App

Ensure you have the latest version of the Instagram app installed on your device. Regular updates often bring new features and improvements. Open the Instagram app by tapping on its icon on your device's home screen.

Step 2: Navigate to the Camera Interface

Once you're in the Instagram app, you'll need to access the camera interface. This can be done by tapping on the camera icon, typically located in the top-left corner of the screen. Alternatively, you can swipe right from your feed to open the camera directly.

Step 3: Explore the Camera Modes

Upon accessing the camera, you'll notice various modes available at the bottom of the screen. These typically include "Live," "Story," and "Reels." Each mode serves a distinct purpose:

- **Live:** Allows users to go live and broadcast to their followers in real-time.

- **Story:** Enables the creation of temporary photo and video content visible to followers for 24 hours.
- **Reels:** Specifically designed for short-form videos, often set to music, with creative features for enhanced engagement.

Step 4: Locate the "Reels" Option

At the bottom of the screen, among the available camera modes, you'll find the "Reels" option. It is usually represented by a clapperboard icon or another distinctive symbol associated with short videos. Take note of the placement of these options, as they might slightly vary based on app updates.

Step 5: Tap on "Reels"

To select the "Reels" mode, simply tap on the "Reels" option at the bottom of the screen. This action will switch the camera interface to Reels mode, preparing the platform for the creation of short, engaging videos.

Step 6: Familiarize Yourself with Reels Features

Once you've selected Reels, take a moment to familiarize yourself with the features available in this mode. Instagram provides various tools to enhance your video creation experience:

- **Music:** Add background music to your Reel from a vast library of tracks.

- **Text and Stickers:** Enhance your video with text overlays, emojis, and stickers.
- **Timer and Countdown:** Use the timer for hands-free recording and the countdown feature for better timing.
- **Speed Control:** Adjust the speed of your video clips for creative effects.
- **Align Tool:** Ensure seamless transitions between clips by using the align tool.

Step 7: Begin Creating Your Reel

With Reels selected and features understood, you can start creating your short video content. Press and hold the capture button to record clips, and utilize the available tools to add creativity to your Reel.

Step 8: Preview and Edit

Before sharing your Reel, take advantage of the preview feature. This allows you to review your video and make any necessary edits. Ensure that the timing, transitions, and added elements meet your expectations.

Step 9: Choose a Cover Photo

Select a cover photo for your Reel. This image will serve as the thumbnail that users see before playing your video. Instagram provides options to choose a frame from your Reel or upload a custom cover.

Step 10: Add a Caption and Share

After finalizing your Reel, add a caption and any relevant hashtags. Choose where you want to share your Reel – whether in your feed, on the Explore page, or both. Finally, tap the "Share" button to publish your Reel.

Conclusion

Selecting Reels on Instagram involves accessing the camera interface, locating the "Reels" option among other modes, and tapping to switch to Reels mode. Once in Reels, explore the creative features available, start recording your short video, and use the editing tools to enhance your content. Following these steps will help you seamlessly navigate to Reels and make the most of this engaging feature on Instagram. Keep in mind that Instagram's interface and features may evolve, so staying updated with any changes is recommended.

4.Recording and Editing

Introduction

Recording and editing Instagram Reels involve utilizing the platform's camera features to create engaging short videos. Instagram provides a user-friendly interface with various tools to enhance creativity, including music, text, stickers, and drawings. This guide will walk you through the steps of recording video clips, adding creative elements, and making the most of the Reels editing features.

Step 1: Access the Reels Mode

Before diving into recording and editing, ensure you are in the Reels mode. Navigate to the camera interface on Instagram and select "Reels" at the bottom of the screen. This will set the stage for creating your short-form video content.

Step 2: Recording Video Clips

In Reels mode, you can record multiple video clips to create a compilation of up to 60 seconds. Follow these steps to capture your video:

Hold Down the Capture Button:

- To start recording, press and hold down the capture button. This button is typically located at the bottom center of the screen.
- The recording begins, and you can continue holding the button to capture a continuous video.

Capture Multiple Clips:

- Lift your finger to stop recording after capturing the first clip.
- To record additional clips for your Reel, tap and hold the capture button again for each new segment.
- Instagram allows you to create a sequence of clips, stitching them together to form your 60-second Reel.

Use the Timer for Hands-Free Recording:

- To simplify the recording process, utilize the timer feature. Set the desired duration for each clip, and the camera will automatically stop recording when the time is up.

Step 3: Adding Creative Elements

Instagram Reels provides a variety of creative elements to enhance your videos. Explore these features to make your content more engaging and visually appealing:

Music:

- Tap on the music note icon to access Instagram's extensive music library. Choose a track that complements your Reel and adds a dynamic element to your video.

Text and Stickers:

- Enhance your Reel with text overlays, emojis, and stickers.
- Tap the "Aa" icon to add text. You can customize the font, color, and placement of the text.
- Access stickers by tapping the smiley face icon. Choose from a wide range of options, including GIFs, emojis, and location-based stickers.

Drawings:

- Express your creativity by adding drawings to your Reel.
- Tap the pen icon to access the drawing tools. Select a color and draw directly on your video.

- Use this feature to highlight elements, create doodles, or add artistic touches.

Step 4: Music and Audio

Adding music to your Reel can significantly enhance its appeal. Here's how to incorporate music into your short video:

Selecting Music:
- Tap the music note icon.
- Browse through Instagram's music library or search for a specific track.
- Choose the portion of the song you want to include in your Reel.

Adjusting Volume:
- You can control the volume of the added music using the volume slider.
- Ensure that the music complements your video content without overpowering other audio elements.

Step 5: Text and Stickers

Text and stickers are powerful tools to convey messages, add context, or inject humor into your Reels. Here's how to use them effectively:

Adding Text:
- Tap the "Aa" icon to open the text tool.

- Enter your desired text and customize its appearance using the available options.
- Drag and resize the text box to place it where you want in your video.

Using Stickers:

- Access stickers by tapping the smiley face icon.
- Explore a wide range of stickers, including emojis, GIFs, and Instagram's curated collection.
- Drag and drop stickers onto your video and adjust their size and position.

Step 6: Timer and Countdown

The timer and countdown features in Instagram Reels make it easier to capture hands-free content with precise timing. Here's how to use these features:

Setting the Timer:

- Tap the clock icon to access the timer feature.
- Set the duration for each clip, and the camera will automatically stop recording when the timer reaches zero.

Countdown:

- The countdown feature provides a visual cue, showing the remaining time before recording starts.

- Use countdown to prepare for each clip and ensure seamless transitions.

Step 7: Speed Control

Adjusting the speed of your video clips can add creative effects and enhance the overall dynamic of your Reel. Follow these steps to control the speed:

Speed Adjustment:
- Tap the speedometer icon to access the speed control feature.
- Choose from options like slow motion or fast forward to create engaging visual effects.

Step 8: Align Tool

To ensure smooth transitions between clips, use the align tool. This feature helps maintain continuity in your Reel. Here's how to utilize the align tool:

Aligning Clips:
- After recording a clip, tap the align tool.
- The previous clip will appear as a transparent overlay, allowing you to align the next clip seamlessly.

Step 9: Preview and Edit

Before sharing your Reel, take advantage of the preview feature to review your video. This allows you to make any necessary edits and ensure your content meets your creative vision.

Step 10: Choose a Cover Photo

Selecting an appealing cover photo is essential as it serves as the thumbnail for your Reel. Here's how to choose a cover photo:

Choosing a Cover:

- After editing your Reel, tap the cover icon.
- Select a frame from your Reel or upload a custom image as the cover photo.

Step 11: Share Your Reel

After recording, editing, and finalizing your Reel, it's time to share it with your followers and the Instagram community. Here's how to share your Reel:

Caption and Hashtags:

- Add a caption that provides context or engages your audience.
- Include relevant hashtags to increase the discoverability of your Reel.

Choose Sharing Options:

- Decide where to share your Reel. You can choose to post it to your feed, share it on the Explore page, or both.

Tap "Share":

- Finally, tap the "Share" button to publish your Reel.

Conclusion

Recording and editing Instagram Reels involve a combination of capturing engaging video clips and leveraging creative elements such as music, text, stickers, and drawings. Instagram provides a user-friend y platform with intuitive tools to make the process seamless and enjoyable. By following the steps outlined in this guide, you can create compellir g Reels that resonate with your audience and showcase your creativi:y. Experiment with different features, explore new music options, and let your imagination run wild to make the most of the 60-second Reel format on Instagram. Keep in mind that Instagram's features may evolve, so staying updated with any changes is recommended.

5.Music and Audio

Introduction

Music is a powerful component in creating captivating Instagram Reels. It adds rhythm, emotion, and an extra layer of creativity to your short videos. Whether you choose a track from Instagram's extensive music library or use your original audio, integrating music into your Reel can elevate its impact and engagement.

Step 1: Access the Reels Mode

Before delving into the music and audio elements, ensure you are in the Reels mode on Instagram. Open the Instagram app, tap on the camera icon, and select "Reels" from the camera mode options at the bottom of the screen.

Step 2: Open the Music Library

To add music to your Reel, tap on the music note icon, usually located among the creative tools. This action opens Instagram's music library, providing a vast collection of tracks across various genres.

Step 3: Choose a Song from the Instagram Music Library

Once you're in the music library, follow these steps to select a song for your Reel:

Explore and Search:

- Explore the curated sections or use the search bar to find a specific song or artist.
- Instagram's music library is regularly updated, offering a diverse range of tracks.

Preview Songs:

- Tap on a song to preview it before adding it to your Reel.
- Previewing helps you choose a track that complements the mood and theme of your video.

Select a Portion of the Song:

- For Reels, you can choose a specific portion of the song that aligns with your video's duration.
- Use the slider to select the segment of the song you want to include in your Reel.

Adjust Volume:

- After choosing a song, you can adjust the volume using the volume slider.
- Ensure the music enhances your video without overpowering other audio elements.

Step 4: Using Your Original Audio

Instagram also allows you to use your original audio or sound in Reels. This is a great option for creators who want to add a personal touch or showcase their own music. Here's how to use your original audio:

Record Your Original Audio:

- While in Reels mode, record a video or segment where you want to use your original audio.
- Speak, sing, or create any audio content that you want to incorporate into your Reel.

Access the Original Audio:

- After recording, tap on the speaker icon at the top of the screen to access your original audio.

- Your recorded audio will be listed, and you can select it for your Reel.

Adjust Audio Settings:

- Just like with the music library, you can adjust the volume of your original audio using the volume slider.
- Ensure the balance between your original audio and other elements in your Reel.

Step 5: Mixing Music and Original Audio

In some cases, creators may want to use a combination of both Instagram's music library and their original audio in a Reel. This can add a unique and personalized touch to the video. Here's how you can mix music and original audio:

Record with Original Audio:

- Record a segment of your Reel using your original audio.

Switch to Music Library:

- For another segment, switch to the music library and select a song.

Adjust Transitions:

- Pay attention to transitions between segments with different audio elements.
- Use the align tool to ensure seamless transitions and maintain a cohesive flow.

Step 6: Preview Your Reel

Before finalizing your Reel, take advantage of the preview feature. This allows you to review your video with the added music or original audio, ensuring it aligns with your creative vision. Previewing helps you catch any potential issues and make adjustments before sharing.

Step 7: Adjusting Volume and Fade

Instagram provides additional controls for adjusting the volume and adding a fade effect to your audio. Here's how you can utilize these features:

Volume Adjustment:

- Tap on the volume icon to access volume controls.
- Adjust the volume levels for the overall audio in your Reel, balancing music, original audio, and any other sounds.

Fade Effect:

- To add a fade effect to your audio, tap on the fade icon.
- This feature gradually increases or decreases the volume, providing smooth transitions between audio segments.

Step 8: Adding Lyrics to Your Reel

For certain songs available in Instagram's music library, you have the option to add lyrics to your Reel. Here's how you can incorporate lyrics:

Access Lyrics:

- After selecting a song, tap on the lyrics icon (usually represented by a small square with text inside).

Choose Lyrics Style:

- Instagram provides various styles for displaying lyrics. Select the one that suits your preference.

Adjust Placement:

- You can adjust the placement of the lyrics on the screen by dragging and dropping the text box.

Preview and Edit:

- Preview your Reel with lyrics to ensure they complement your video.
- Make any necessary adjustments to the lyrics' appearance and placement.

Step 9: Finalize Your Reel

Once you are satisfied with the music or original audio, volume settings, and any additional elements like lyrics, you are ready to finalize your Reel. Proceed to the next steps to add a cover photo, caption, and share your creation with your followers.

Step 10: Add a Cover Photo

Before sharing your Reel, choose a cover photo. This is the thumbnail that users will see before playing your video. Here's how to add a cover photo:

Tap the Cover Icon:

- After editing your Reel, tap on the cover icon (usually represented by a square with mountains).

Choose a Frame or Upload a Custom Cover:

- Instagram automatically suggests frames from your Reel. Select one that represents your video well.
- Alternatively, you can upload a custom image as the cover.

Step 11: Add a Caption and Share Your Reel

After finalizing your Reel, add a caption that provides context or engages your audience. You can also include relevant hashtags to increase the discoverability of your video. Choose where you want to share your Reel – whether in your feed, on the Explore page, or both. Finally, tap the "Share" button to publish your Reel.

Conclusion

Adding music to your Instagram Reel is a dynamic way to enhance the visual experience and engage your audience. Whether you choose a track from Instagram's music library or incorporate your original audio, the platform provides versatile tools for creative expression. Experiment with different songs, explore the possibilities of mixing music and original audio, and use additional features like lyrics to make your Reels stand out. By following the steps outlined in this guide, you can seamlessly integrate music into your Reels and create captivating short-form videos that resonate with your audience. Keep in mind that Instagram's features may evolve, so staying updated with any changes is recommended.

6.Text and Stickers

Introduction

Text and stickers are powerful tools in Instagram Reels that allow you to add context, captions, emojis, and other visual elements to your short videos. These features not only enhance the storytelling aspect of your Reel but also contribute to the overall creativity and engagement. This guide will provide a detailed walkthrough on how to use text and stickers in your Reel.

Step 1: Access the Reels Mode

To get started, ensure you are in the Reels mode on Instagram. Open the Instagram app, tap on the camera icon, and select "Reels" from the camera mode options at the bottom of the screen.

Step 2: Record Your Reel

Before adding text and stickers, record the main content of your Reel. This can be a series of video clips capturing different moments or a continuous video sequence. Once you've recorded your content, you're ready to enhance it with text and stickers.

Step 3: Access the Text Tool

To add text to your Reel, tap on the "Aa" icon, which represents the text tool. This will open the text editing options, allowing you to input and customize your text.

Step 4: Add Captions and Messages

Here's how to effectively use the text tool to add captions and messages to your Reel:

Enter Your Text:

- Tap the area provided for text input and type your caption or message.
- You can add multiple text boxes for different segments of your Reel.

Customize Text Appearance:

- Instagram provides options to customize your text's appearance, including font style, size, and color.
- Experiment with different styles to find the one that complements your video.

Text Placement:

- Drag and drop the text boxes to position them where you want in your Reel.
- Ensure that the text doesn't obstruct crucial elements in your video.

Step 5: Add Emojis

Emojis are a fun and expressive way to convey emotions and add personality to your Reel. Here's how to incorporate emojis:

Access Emojis:

- Tap on the smiley face icon to access the emoji library.
- Instagram provides a diverse collection of emojis, including smileys, animals, objects, and more.

Choose Emojis:

- Select the emojis that fit the mood or theme of your Reel.
- You can mix and match emojis to create a playful or expressive vibe.

Emoji Placement:

- Drag and drop the chosen emojis onto your video.
- Experiment with different placements to find the most engaging positions.

Step 6: Use Stickers

Stickers are versatile visual elements that can add creativity and flair to your Reel. Here's how to use stickers effectively:

Access Stickers:

- Tap on the smiley face icon again to access the sticker library.

- Instagram offers a wide range of stickers, including GIFs, location-based stickers, date and time stickers, and more.

Choose Stickers:

- Explore the sticker options and choose the ones that complement your video.
- Consider the theme and message of your Reel when selecting stickers.

Sticker Placement:

- Similar to emojis, drag and drop the stickers onto your video.
- Resize and reposition stickers to enhance visual appeal.

Step 7: Add Drawings and Doodles

If you want to add a personal touch or highlight specific elements in your Reel, you can use the drawing tool. Here's how to add drawings and doodles:

Access the Drawing Tool:

- Tap on the pen icon to access the drawing tools.
- Instagram provides various brush styles, colors, and sizes for drawing.

Draw on Your Video:

- Choose a brush style and color, then draw directly on your video.

- Use this feature to create doodles, highlight objects, or add artistic touches.

Eraser Tool:

- If you make a mistake, the eraser tool allows you to undo or correct your drawings.

Step 8: Customize Text and Stickers for Each Clip

If your Reel consists of multiple clips, you can customize text and stickers for each segment. Here's how to maintain consistency and creativity across different clips:

Use the Align Tool:

- After recording a clip, use the align tool to ensure a smooth transition to the next segment.
- This tool helps maintain the placement and continuity of text and stickers.

Change Text and Stickers:

- Before recording each clip, go back to the text and sticker options.
- Adjust or change text and stickers to suit the content of the new clip.

Step 9: Preview and Edit

Before finalizing your Reel, take advantage of the preview feature. This allows you to review your video with added text, stickers, and other elements. Previewing helps you ensure that the text is readable, stickers are well-placed, and the overall visual appeal meets your creative vision.

Step 10: Adjust Text and Sticker Duration

Instagram allows you to control the duration of text and stickers in your Reel. Here's how to adjust their duration:

Tap on the Text or Sticker:

- During the preview, tap on the text or sticker you want to adjust.

Set Duration:

- Use the handles on the timeline to adjust the duration of the text or sticker.
- Ensure that the duration aligns with the specific segment of your Reel.

Step 11: Finalize Your Reel

After adding text, stickers, and other creative elements to your Reel, you're ready to finalize your video. Proceed to the next steps to add a cover photo, caption, and share your creation with your followers.

Step 12: Add a Cover Photo

Choose a cover photo for your Reel before sharing it. Here's how to add a cover photo:

Tap the Cover Icon:

- After editing your Reel, tap on the cover icon (usually represented by a square with mountains).

Choose a Frame or Upload a Custom Cover:

- Instagram automatically suggests frames from your Reel. Select one that represents your video well.
- Alternatively, you can upload a custom image as the cover.

Step 13: Add a Caption and Share Your Reel

After finalizing your Reel with text, stickers, and cover photo, add a caption that provides context or engages your audience. Include relevant hashtags to increase the discoverability of your video. Choose where you want to share your Reel – whether in your feed, on the Explore page, or both. Finally, tap the "Share" button to publish your Reel.

Conclusion

Adding text and stickers to your Instagram Reel is an effective way to enhance storytelling, convey messages, and add a creative flair to your short videos. By following the steps outlined in this guide, you can use text, emojis, stickers, and drawings to create engaging and visually appealing Reels. Experiment with different styles, explore the extensive library of stickers and emojis, and use the drawing tools to personalize your content. Keep in mind that Instagram's features may evolve, so staying updated with any changes is recommended.

7.Timer and Countdown

Introduction

The timer and countdown features in Instagram Reels are designed to enhance the content creation experience by allowing users to record hands-free. These features are particularly useful for maintaining a steady shot, achieving precise timing, and ensuring seamless transitions between clips. This guide will walk you through the steps of using the timer and countdown features in Reels, providing valuable insights into their applications and benefits.

Step 1: Access the Reels Mode

Before diving into the timer and countdown features, ensure you are in the Reels mode on Instagram. Open the Instagram app, tap on the camera icon, and select "Reels" from the camera mode options at the bottom of the screen.

Step 2: Set Up Your Shot

Before using the timer and countdown, position your camera and frame your shot according to your creative vision. Ensure that your camera is stable, and you have the desired composition for your Reel.

Step 3: Access the Timer Feature

To access the timer feature in Instagram Reels, follow these steps:

Tap on the Clock Icon:

- Look for the clock icon, usually located among the creative tools on the left side of the screen.
- Tapping on the clock icon opens the timer settings.

Set the Timer Duration:

- Choose the desired duration for each segment of your Reel.
- The timer allows you to set the duration for hands-free recording, eliminating the need to hold down the capture button.

Step 4: Utilize the Countdown Feature

Once you've set the timer, the countdown feature ensures a smooth transition between setting up your shot and the actual recording. Here's how to utilize the countdown:

Tap on the Countdown Icon:

- Look for the countdown icon, usually represented by a circle with numbers counting down.
- Tapping on the countdown icon initiates the countdown sequence.

Countdown Duration:

- The countdown typically lasts a few seconds, giving you time to prepare for recording.
- This feature ensures that your Reel begins recording precisely when the timer reaches zero.

Step 5: Start Recording Hands-Free

With the timer and countdown set up, you are ready to start recording hands-free. Here's how the process unfolds:

Wait for the Countdown:
- Once you tap the countdown icon, the numbers will start counting down.
- Use this time to get into position and prepare for the hands-free recording.

Hands-Free Recording:
- When the countdown reaches zero, Instagram will start recording based on the timer duration you set.
- You can focus on your performance, movement, or any other creative element without having to hold down the capture button.

Step 6: Benefits of Hands-Free Recording

Hands-free recording with the timer and countdown features offers several advantages for content creators:

Steady Shots:
- Without the need to hold the capture button, creators can achieve steadier shots, reducing the risk of shaky footage.

Precise Timing:

- The timer allows for precise timing in each segment of your Reel. This is particularly useful for choreographed performances, tutorials, or any content that requires specific timing.

Freedom of Movement:

- Creators have the freedom to move around or focus on their performance without being tethered to holding down the capture button.

Consistent Segments:

- Using the timer and countdown ensures that each segment of your Reel has a consistent duration, contributing to a polished and well-paced video.

Step 7: Use Timer for Different Reel Segments

If your Reel consists of multiple segments or scenes, you can use the timer for each one. This allows for a cohesive and well-organized video with consistent timing. Follow these steps to use the timer for different Reel segments:

Record First Segment:

- Set the timer for the duration of the first segment and record the hands-free footage.

Stop Recording:

- Lift your finger to stop recording the first segment.

Adjust Timer for Next Segment:

- Before recording the next segment, adjust the timer duration based on the desired length for that particular scene.

Repeat the Process:

- Repeat the process for each subsequent segment, ensuring that each has its own designated timer duration.

Step 8: Combine Timer with Creative Elements

The timer and countdown features can be combined with other creative elements in Instagram Reels for a more dynamic and engaging video. Consider using the timer in conjunction with music, text, stickers, and other features to enhance the overall viewer experience.

Step 9: Align Tool for Seamless Transitions

To ensure seamless transitions between clips recorded with the timer, use the align tool. This feature helps maintain continuity and smooth flow in your Reel. Here's how to use the align tool:

Record First Segment:

- After recording the first segment with the timer, tap on the align tool.

Review Overlay:

- The previous clip will appear as a transparent overlay on your screen.

- Use this overlay to align the next segment seamlessly.

Repeat for Each Segment:

- Repeat the process for each subsequent segment, using the align tool to create a polished and cohesive Reel.

Step 10: Preview and Edit

Before finalizing your Reel, take advantage of the preview feature. This allows you to review your video with hands-free recording, timer, and other creative elements. Previewing helps you ensure that each segment aligns seamlessly, and the overall video meets your creative vision.

Step 11: Finalize Your Reel

Once you are satisfied with the hands-free recording, timer settings, and overall content of your Reel, proceed to finalize your video. Add a cover photo, caption, and any additional elements to make your Reel visually appealing and engaging.

Conclusion

The timer and countdown features in Instagram Reels provide creators with a valuable tool for hands-free recording, precise timing, and seamless transitions between segments. By following the steps outlined in this guide, you can leverage these features to enhance the quality and professionalism of your short-form videos. Whether you're creating dance performances, tutorials, or any content that requires specific timing, the timer and countdown features contribute to a smooth and polished Reel. Keep in mind that Instagram's features may evolve, so staying updated with any changes is recommended.

8.Speed Control

Introduction

Speed control is a versatile tool in Instagram Reels that empowers creators to manipulate the pace of their video clips. Whether you want to create slow-motion sequences for emphasis or speed up dynamic moments, this feature adds a layer of creativity to your short-form videos. This guide will provide a detailed walkthrough on how to adjust the speed of your Reel, exploring the various options, creative applications, and tips for achieving engaging visual effects.

Step 1: Access the Reels Mode

Before delving into speed control, ensure you are in the Reels mode on Instagram. Open the Instagram app, tap on the camera icon, and select "Reels" from the camera mode options at the bottom of the screen.

Step 2: Record Your Reel

Before adjusting the speed of your video clips, record the main content of your Reel. This can be a series of video clips capturing different moments or a continuous video sequence. Once you've recorded your content, you're ready to enhance it with speed control.

Step 3: Access the Speed Control Feature

To adjust the speed of your video clips in Instagram Reels, follow these steps:

Tap on the Speedometer Icon:

- Look for the speedometer icon, usually located among the creative tools on the left side of the screen.
- Tapping on the speedometer icon opens the speed control settings.

Select Speed Options:

- Instagram provides various speed options, allowing you to choose between slow motion, regular speed, and fast motion.
- Common options include 0.3x (slow motion), 1x (regular speed), and 3x (fast motion).

Step 4: Adjust Speed for Each Clip

After accessing the speed control feature, you can adjust the speed for each specific video clip in your Reel. Here's how:

Choose a Clip:

- Tap on the video clip you want to adjust.

- Instagram allows you to apply different speeds to individual clips within the same Reel.

Select Speed Option:

- Once you've chosen a clip, select the desired speed option. You can experiment with different speeds to achieve the desired visual effect.

Repeat for Other Clips:

- Repeat the process for each video clip in your Reel, adjusting the speed based on the pacing you want to create.

Step 5: Creative Applications of Speed Control

Speed control in Instagram Reels opens up a range of creative possibilities for content creators:

Slow Motion for Emphasis:

- Use slow motion (e.g., 0.3x) to emphasize specific moments in your Reel.
- Slow-motion clips can add drama, highlight details, or create a dreamy, cinematic feel.

Fast Motion for Dynamic Sequences:

- Speed up clips (e.g., 2x or 3x) to create dynamic and energetic sequences.
- Fast motion is effective for showcasing rapid movements, quick transitions, or enhancing the overall tempo of your Reel.

Mixing Speeds for Variety:

- Experiment with a combination of slow-motion and fast-motion clips to add variety and keep your audience engaged.
- Mixing speeds can create a dynamic and visually interesting Reel.

Narrative Pacing:

- Adjusting the speed based on the narrative of your Reel can enhance storytelling.
- Speed up the pacing during action sequences and slow down for more contemplative or emotional moments.

Step 6: Use Speed Control for Transitions

Speed control is not only about changing the pace of individual clips but also about creating seamless transitions between them. Here's how to use speed control for transitions:

Overlap Clips:

- When adjusting the speed of a clip, consider overlapping it with the preceding or following clip.
- Overlapping helps create smooth transitions and avoids abrupt changes in speed.

Gradual Changes:

- Instead of applying speed changes abruptly, consider gradually increasing or decreasing the speed.

- Gradual changes contribute to a more natural and visually pleasing transition.

Experiment with Speed Ramps:

- Create speed ramps by gradually increasing or decreasing the speed within a single clip.
- Speed ramps can add a dynamic element to your Reel, especially during transitions between scenes.

Step 7: Preview and Adjust

Before finalizing your Reel, use the preview feature to review the impact of the speed adjustments. This allows you to ensure that the pacing, transitions, and overall flow of your video meet your creative vision. Make any necessary adjustments to achieve the desired effect.

Step 8: Combine Speed Control with Other Features

Enhance the visual appeal of your Reel by combining speed control with other creative elements. Consider using music, text, stickers, and filters to complement the speed adjustments and create a cohesive and engaging video.

Step 9: Align Tool for Smooth Transitions

To maintain smooth transitions between clips with different speeds, use the align tool. This feature overlays the previous clip as a transparent guide, helping you align the next clip seamlessly. Here's how to use the align tool:

Record First Segment:

- After adjusting the speed of the first clip, tap on the align tool.

Review Overlay:

- The previous clip will appear as a transparent overlay on your screen.
- Use this overlay to align the next clip seamlessly.

Repeat for Each Segment:

- Repeat the process for each subsequent segment, using the align tool to ensure a polished and cohesive Reel.

Step 10: Preview and Edit

Before sharing your Reel, take advantage of the preview feature to review the final result. Check the overall pacing, transitions, and visual effects achieved through speed control. Make any final edits to perfect your Reel.

Step 11: Finalize Your Reel

Once you are satisfied with the speed adjustments, transitions, and overall content of your Reel, proceed to finalize your video. Add a cover photo, caption, and any additional elements to make your Reel visually appealing and engaging.

Conclusion

Speed control in Instagram Reels is a valuable tool that empowers creators to add dynamic and creative effects to their short-form videos. By adjusting the speed of individual clips, experimenting with slow-motion and fast-motion sequences, and combining speed control with other features, you can elevate the visual appeal of your Reel. Whether you're telling a story, showcasing a performance, or sharing a tutorial, speed control offers a versatile and engaging way to captivate your audience. Keep in mind that Instagram's features may evolve, so staying updated with any changes is recommended.

9.Align Tool

Introduction

The align tool in Instagram Reels plays a crucial role in enhancing the overall quality of short-form videos. It addresses the challenge of maintaining continuity between successive clips, ensuring that transitions are seamless and visually appealing. This guide will provide a detailed walkthrough on the importance of the align tool, the steps to use it effectively, and practical tips for achieving polished transitions in your Reels.

Step 1: Access the Reels Mode

Before exploring the align tool, ensure you are in the Reels mode on Instagram. Open the Instagram app, tap on the camera icon, and select "Reels" from the camera mode options at the bottom of the screen.

Step 2: Record Your Reel

Before utilizing the align tool, record the main content of your Reel. This can include a series of video clips capturing different moments or a continuous video sequence. Once you've recorded your content, you're ready to enhance it with the align tool.

Step 3: Understand the Importance of Alignment

Seamless transitions between successive clips contribute significantly to the overall visual appeal of a Reel. The align tool becomes crucial in achieving this by addressing potential discrepancies in the positioning of objects, subjects, or the overall composition between clips. Maintaining alignment ensures that the viewer experiences a fluid and uninterrupted narrative, enhancing the professionalism and engagement of your Reel.

Step 4: Access the Align Tool

To access the align tool in Instagram Reels, follow these steps:

Record Your First Segment:
- After recording your first clip, tap on the align tool icon, which is typically located among the creative tools on the left side of the screen.

Review Overlay:
- The align tool overlays the previous clip as a transparent guide on your screen.

- This overlay helps you align the next clip seamlessly with the preceding one.

Step 5: Align Successive Clips

Once you've accessed the align tool and reviewed the overlay of the previous clip, you can align successive clips to create a smooth transition. Here's how:

Record the Next Segment:
- After using the align tool, record the next segment of your Reel.
- The align tool overlay serves as a guide to help you position the next clip in alignment with the previous one.

Use Overlay as a Reference:
- Pay attention to key elements, objects, or subjects in the overlay as you record the next segment.
- Align these elements with the corresponding features in the live view to ensure continuity.

Repeat for Each Successive Clip:
- Repeat the process for each subsequent clip in your Reel, utilizing the align tool to maintain continuity and alignment between segments.

Step 6: Gradual Transitions with the Align Tool

The align tool is not only about maintaining static alignment but also about creating gradual transitions. Here's how you can achieve gradual transitions using the align tool:

Overlapping Clips:

- Overlap the end of the first clip with the beginning of the next clip.
- This overlap provides room for gradual transitions, making the alignment process smoother.

Use Align Tool for Overlapping Section:

- When using the align tool, pay attention to the overlapping section.
- Align the features in this section to ensure a gradual and seamless transition between the clips.

Check for Fluid Motion:

- Preview the Reel to ensure that the overlapping section creates a fluid and visually pleasing transition.
- Adjust the alignment as needed to achieve the desired effect.

Step 7: Experiment with Different Transitions

The align tool offers flexibility in creating various types of transitions. Experiment with different styles to add visual interest to your Reel:

Slide Transitions:

- Use the align tool to create slide transitions where one clip smoothly slides into the next.
- This technique works well for Reels with horizontal or vertical movement.

Fade Transitions:
- Achieve fade transitions by aligning clips with gradual changes in opacity.
- Adjust the alignment to create a fading effect between successive clips.

Zoom Transitions:
- Experiment with zoom transitions by aligning clips with incremental changes in zoom levels.
- The align tool helps maintain consistency in the zoom effect.

Step 8: Use Align Tool for Multi-Clip Reels

If your Reel consists of multiple clips, each with its own unique content, the align tool becomes even more valuable. Here's how to use the align tool for multi-clip Reels:

Record First Segment:
- After recording the first clip, use the align tool to ensure a smooth transition to the next clip.

Adjust Alignments for Each Segment:

- Before recording each subsequent clip, adjust the alignment based on the unique content and composition.
- The align tool ensures that each clip seamlessly transitions to the next.

Maintain Consistency:

- Pay attention to consistent elements across clips, such as the position of subjects or key objects.
- Consistency enhances the overall flow and professionalism of your multi-clip Reel.

Step 9: Preview and Adjust

Before finalizing your Reel, use the preview feature to review the transitions created with the align tool. Check for smooth alignments, gradual transitions, and overall visual appeal. Make any necessary adjustments to achieve the desired effect.

Step 10: Combine Align Tool with Other Features

Enhance the visual appeal of your Reel by combining the align tool with other creative elements. Consider using speed control, music, text, stickers, and filters to complement the transitions created with the align tool. A cohesive combination of features contributes to a more engaging and dynamic video.

Step 11: Finalize Your Reel

Once you are satisfied with the transitions, alignments, and overall content of your Reel, proceed to finalize your video. Add a cover photo, caption, and any additional elements to make your Reel visually appealing and engaging.

Conclusion

The align tool in Instagram Reels is an essential feature for creators aiming to achieve seamless transitions and maintain continuity between successive clips. By understanding the significance of alignment, utilizing the align tool effectively, and experimenting with different transition styles, you can elevate the visual appeal and professionalism of your short-form videos. Whether you're creating a single continuous Reel or a multi-clip sequence, the align tool ensures that each segment flows seamlessly into the next, providing a more engaging viewer experience. Keep in mind that Instagram's features may evolve, so staying updated with any changes is recommended.

10.Preview and Edit

Introduction

Previewing and editing your Instagram Reel before sharing it allows you to fine-tune your content, ensuring that it aligns with your creative intentions and captivates your audience. This guide will provide a detailed walkthrough on the significance of previewing, the steps to preview and edit your Reel, and practical tips for making impactful adjustments before sharing your video.

Step 1: Access the Reels Mode

Open the Instagram app on your device, tap on the camera icon, and select "Reels" from the camera mode options at the bottom of the screen. This ensures that you are in the Reels mode, ready to access the preview and editing features.

Step 2: Record Your Reel

Before previewing and editing your Reel, record the main content of your video. This can include a series of clips capturing different moments or a continuous video sequence. Once you've recorded your content, you're ready to proceed to the preview and editing steps.

Step 3: Understand the Importance of Previewing

Previewing your Reel is a crucial step in the content creation process. It allows you to:

Assess Visual Flow:

- Check the overall visual flow and pacing of your Reel.
- Ensure that transitions between clips are smooth and contribute to a cohesive viewing experience.

Review Content Quality:

- Evaluate the quality of your video content, including clarity, lighting, and composition.
- Identify any areas that may need improvement or adjustment.

Verify Timing and Alignment:

- Confirm that the timing of each clip aligns with your creative intentions.
- Use the align tool to ensure seamless transitions between successive clips.

Check for Consistency:

- Ensure consistency in visual elements, such as text, stickers, and other creative additions.
- Verify that the overall style and tone of your Reel remain consistent throughout.

Step 4: Access the Preview Feature

To preview your Reel, follow these steps:

Tap on the Preview Icon:

- Look for the preview icon, which is usually represented by an eye or play button.
- Tapping on this icon allows you to review your Reel before finalizing and sharing it.

Step 5: Review Your Reel

Once you've accessed the preview feature, take the time to review your Reel. Pay attention to the following aspects:

Visual Flow:

- Watch the entire Reel to assess the flow of content from start to finish.
- Check for any abrupt transitions or pacing issues.

Content Quality:

- Evaluate the visual and audio quality of your video content.
- Look for any areas that may need improvement, such as adjusting lighting or enhancing clarity.

Timing and Alignment:

- Verify that the timing and alignment of each clip align with your creative vision.
- Use the align tool to address any discrepancies in transitions.

Consistency in Style:

- Ensure that any added elements, such as text, stickers, or filters, contribute to a consistent and appealing style.
- Make adjustments if certain elements appear out of place or disrupt the overall aesthetic.

Step 6: Use the Edit Feature

If you identify areas that need improvement during the preview, you can use the edit feature to make necessary adjustments. Follow these steps:

Tap on the Edit Icon:

- Look for the edit icon, which is often represented by a pencil or edit button.
- Tapping on this icon opens the editing options for your Reel.

Access Editing Tools:

- Explore the available editing tools, which may include options for trimming, adjusting clip speed, adding music, and more.
- Select the tool that addresses the specific aspect you want to edit.

Step 7: Make Necessary Adjustments

Based on your review and the aspects you want to improve, make the necessary adjustments using the editing tools. Here are some common adjustments you might consider:

Trim Clips:

- Use the trimming tool to adjust the duration of specific clips.
- Trim excess footage or refine the timing of certain moments.

Adjust Clip Speed:

- If needed, use the speed control feature to adjust the speed of individual clips.
- This can enhance the pacing and overall dynamic of your Reel.

Add or Edit Music:

- If your Reel includes music, ensure that the soundtrack complements the content.
- Adjust the volume or consider changing the music if it doesn't align with your creative vision.

Fine-Tune Visual Elements:

- Refine the placement of text, stickers, or other visual elements to achieve a polished look.
- Ensure that these elements enhance rather than distract from the overall content.

Step 8: Preview Again

After making adjustments using the editing tools, tap on the preview icon again to review your Reel. This additional preview allows you to confirm that your edits have had the desired impact and improved the overall quality of your video.

Step 9: Iterative Editing

Previewing and editing your Reel can be an iterative process. If, during the second preview, you identify additional areas for improvement, return to the editing tools and make further adjustments. Continue this process until you are satisfied with the final result.

Step 10: Pay Attention to Details

As you preview and edit, pay attention to the finer details that can elevate the professionalism of your Reel:

Color Correction:

- Use editing tools to adjust the color balance and enhance the overall visual appeal.
- Correct any color inconsistencies or lighting issues.

Text Legibility:

- Ensure that any text or captions added to your Reel are legible and complement the visual elements.
- Adjust font size, color, or placement as needed.

Transitions:

- Check that transitions between clips are seamless and contribute to a cohesive narrative.
- Address any sudden jumps or disruptions in the flow.

Step 11: Add Final Touches

Before finalizing your Reel, consider adding any final touches that enhance its overall appeal:

Cover Photo:

- Choose a visually appealing cover photo for your Reel.
- The cover photo is the first impression viewers will have, so make it engaging.

Caption and Hashtags:

- Craft a compelling caption that provides context or engages your audience.
- Include relevant hashtags to increase the discoverability of your Reel.

Step 12: Share Your Reel

Once you are satisfied with the preview and editing process, proceed to share your Reel. Choose whether you want to share it on your profile, in your story, or both. Tap the "Share" button to make your Reel visible to your followers and potentially reach a wider audience on the Explore page.

Conclusion

Previewing and editing your Instagram Reel before sharing it is a critical step in ensuring that your content aligns with your creative vision and engages your audience effectively. By taking the time to review the visual flow, assess content quality, and make necessary adjustments using the editing tools, you can refine your Reel for optimal impact. Paying attention to details, iterating through the preview and editing process, and adding final touches contribute to the overall professionalism and appeal of your short-form video. Keep in mind that Instagram's features may evolve, so staying updated with any changes is recommended.

11.Add a Cover

Introduction

The cover photo of your Instagram Reel serves as the thumbnail that viewers see before deciding to play your video. This visual preview is an opportunity to make a strong first impression and pique the interest of potential viewers. This guide will explore the significance of choosing an appealing cover, the steps to add a cover to your Reel, and practical tips for creating a captivating thumbnail.

Step 1: Access the Reels Mode

Open the Instagram app on your device, tap on the camera icon, and select "Reels" from the camera mode options at the bottom of the screen. Ensure that you are in the Reels mode to proceed with the cover photo selection.

Step 2: Record Your Reel

Before adding a cover photo, record the main content of your Reel. This can include a series of clips capturing different moments, a continuous video sequence, or any other creative content you intend to share. Once you've recorded your content, you're ready to choose a cover photo.

Step 3: Importance of a Captivating Cover

The cover photo of your Reel is the first visual element that potential viewers encounter. Its importance lies in:

First Impressions:

- The cover photo is the initial impression viewers have of your Reel.
- A captivating cover can entice viewers to click and play your video.

Visual Preview:

- It provides a visual preview of the content within your Reel.
- Viewers decide whether to engage based on the thumbnail, making it a key factor in attracting attention.

Branding Opportunity:

- The cover photo is an opportunity to reinforce your brand or personal style.
- Consistent and visually appealing covers contribute to a cohesive aesthetic on your profile.

Step 4: Access the Cover Photo Feature

After recording your Reel, follow these steps to choose a cover photo:

Tap on the Cover Icon:

- Look for the cover icon, often represented by a square with mountains.
- Tapping on this icon opens the cover photo feature.

Step 5: Choose a Frame or Upload Custom Cover

Once you've accessed the cover photo feature, you have two options:

Choose a Frame:

- Instagram automatically suggests frames from your Reel.
- Browse through the suggested frames and select one that best represents your video.

Upload a Custom Cover:

- Alternatively, you can upload a custom image as your cover photo.
- Tap on the option to upload, choose an image from your device, and set it as the cover.

Step 6: Considerations for Choosing a Cover Photo

When selecting a cover photo, consider the following tips to create an appealing thumbnail:

Clear and Vibrant Imagery:

- Choose a cover that features clear and vibrant imagery.
- High-quality visuals make your Reel more enticing to viewers.

Representative of Content:

- Select a cover that accurately represents the content of your Reel.
- Ensure that it provides a glimpse into the theme or key moments of your video.

Engaging Composition:

- Opt for a visually engaging composition.
- Consider elements such as balance, focal points, and color contrast.

Incorporate Branding Elements:

- If applicable, incorporate branding elements into your cover.
- This can include logos, colors, or any consistent visual elements associated with your brand.

Contrast for Visibility:

- Ensure that text or important elements are visible against the background.
- Use contrast to make key details stand out.

Step 7: Adjust the Cover Photo

After choosing a cover photo, you can make adjustments to ensure it aligns perfectly with your vision. Follow these steps:

Tap on the Adjust Icon:

- Look for the adjust icon, often represented by sliders or a tuning fork.
- Tapping on this icon allows you to make adjustments to the positioning and framing of your cover photo.

Use the Slider:

- Adjust the slider to zoom in or out, reposition, or crop the cover photo.
- Ensure that the cover is framed in a visually appealing and balanced manner.

Step 8: Preview the Cover

Before finalizing your cover photo, take the time to preview how it will appear on your profile. This ensures that it meets your expectations and aligns with the overall aesthetic of your Instagram feed.

Step 9: Save Your Cover Photo

Once you are satisfied with the chosen cover photo and any adjustments made, save the changes. This sets the selected image as the thumbnail for your Reel.

Step 10: Additional Tips for Eye-Catching Covers

Consider the following additional tips to enhance the visual appeal of your cover photo:

Dynamic Imagery:

- If your Reel is dynamic and action-packed, choose a cover that reflects this energy.
- Showcase a compelling moment that sparks curiosity.

Emotion and Expression:

- If your Reel conveys emotion or expression, select a cover that captures a poignant or expressive moment.
- Faces and emotions can draw viewers in.

Consistency Across Covers:

- If you create multiple Reels, aim for consistency in your cover photo style.
- This contributes to a cohesive and visually pleasing profile.

Test with Audience:

- Consider testing different cover photos with your audience to see which generates more engagement.
- Monitor analytics to understand viewer preferences.

Step 11: Combine with Captivating Titles

Enhance the impact of your cover photo by combining it with a captivating title or caption. Consider adding text directly on the cover or crafting a compelling title that complements the visual appeal. The combination of an engaging cover and an intriguing title can significantly increase viewer interest.

Step 12: Share Your Reel

Once you've chosen an appealing cover photo and added any additional elements, you're ready to share your Reel. Tap the "Share" button to make your video visible to your followers and potentially reach a broader audience on the Explore page.

Conclusion

Choosing an engaging cover photo for your Instagram Reel is a crucial step in capturing viewer attention and encouraging them to engage with your content. By understanding the importance of a captivating cover, following the steps to add a cover to your Reel, and implementing practical tips for creating an eye-catching thumbnail, you can make a strong first impression on your audience. The cover photo serves as a visual gateway to your Reel, and a well-chosen thumbnail can significantly contribute to the overall success of your short-form video. Keep in mind that Instagram's features may evolve, so staying updated with any changes is recommended.

12.Share Your Reel

Introduction

After creating a compelling Reel, the next crucial step is sharing it with your audience. This involves adding a caption, relevant hashtags, and deciding where you want to share your Reel—on your feed, the Explore page, or both. This guide will provide a detailed walkthrough of the sharing process, including the importance of captions and hashtags, and tips for maximizing the reach of your Instagram Reel.

Step 1: Satisfy with Your Reel

Before initiating the sharing process, make sure you are satisfied with your Reel. Review the video, cover photo, and any additional elements to ensure they align with your creative vision and captivate your audience effectively.

Step 2: Tap on the Arrow Button

Once you are satisfied with your Reel, tap on the arrow button. This button is typically located in the bottom right corner of the screen and is the universal indicator for proceeding to the next step in the sharing process.

Step 3: Caption Your Reel

Adding a caption to your Reel is an essential step in providing context, engaging your audience, and encouraging interactions. Follow these steps to caption your Reel:

Tap on the Caption Field:

- The caption field is usually located at the bottom of the screen.
- Tap on the field to enter your caption.

Craft an Engaging Caption:

- Craft a caption that complements your Reel and encourages viewers to engage.
- Consider using emojis, asking questions, or adding a call-to-action to boost interaction.

Use Relevant Keywords:

- Incorporate relevant keywords into your caption to enhance discoverability.
- Think about words or phrases that align with the content and might be commonly searched by your audience.

Keep it Concise:

- While you have a character limit for captions keeping it concise is generally advisable.
- Aim for clarity and impact within the allotted space.

Step 4: Add Hashtags

Including relevant hashtags in your Reel's caption is a powerful strategy for increasing discoverability and reaching a broader audience. Here's how to add hashtags:

Use the Hashtag Symbol:

- Begin your caption with the hashtag symbol (#) to indicate that you are adding hashtags.

Enter Relevant Hashtags:

- Enter relevant hashtags directly in the caption.
- Choose hashtags that are specific to your content, industry, or niche.

Mix Popular and Niche Hashtags:

- Include a mix of popular and niche hashtags to optimize discoverability.

- Popular hashtags may expose your Reel to a larger audience, while niche hashtags target a specific community.

Limit the Number of Hashtags:

- While Instagram allows up to 30 hashtags per post, it's advisable to focus on quality over quantity.
- Aim for a mix of around 5 to 15 relevant hashtags for optimal impact.

Step 5: Choose Where to Share Your Reel

Instagram offers options for sharing your Reel on your feed and/or the Explore page. Here's how to make this decision:

Choose Your Audience:

- Decide whether you want to share your Reel with your existing followers (on your feed) or potentially reach a new audience (on the Explore page).

Select Share on Feed:

- If you choose to share on your feed, your Reel will appear in your profile grid and the feeds of your followers.
- This ensures that your existing audience sees your Reel.

Select Share on Explore Page:

- If you opt to share on the Explore page, your Reel has the potential to reach a broader audience beyond your followers.

- Instagram's algorithm may recommend your Reel to users who have similar interests or engage with content similar to yours.

Choose Both (Feed and Explore):

- For maximum visibility, you can choose to share your Reel on both your feed and the Explore page.

Step 6: Review and Finalize

Before hitting the share button, take a moment to review your Reel, caption, hashtags, and sharing preferences. Ensure everything aligns with your intentions and effectively communicates the message or story you want to convey.

Step 7: Tap on the Share Button

Once you are confident in your Reel and associated details, tap on the share button. This button is typically represented by a paper airplane icon and is located in the bottom right corner of the screen.

Step 8: Engagement and Interaction

After sharing your Reel, monitor engagement and interactions from your audience. Respond to comments, engage with viewers, and track the performance of your Reel using Instagram Insights. This data provides valuable insights into the reach, interactions, and overall impact of your video.

Additional Tips for Optimizing Reel Sharing

Consistent Posting Schedule:

- Establish a consistent posting schedule for your Reels to keep your audience engaged.
- Regular posting increases the likelihood of appearing in your followers' feeds.

Utilize Instagram's Music Library:

- Leverage Instagram's extensive music library to enhance the audio experience of your Reel.
- Choose music that complements the theme or mood of your content.

Engage with Your Audience:

- Actively engage with your audience by responding to comments and direct messages.
- Foster a sense of community around your content.

Experiment with Trends:

- Stay informed about popular trends on Instagram and experiment with incorporating them into your Reels.
- Trendy content is more likely to capture attention and resonate with a broader audience.

Promote Cross-Platform Sharing:

- Share links to your Reels on other social media platforms, blog posts, or newsletters to cross-promote your content.
- This can drive additional traffic to your Instagram profile.

Conclusion

Sharing your Instagram Reel involves more than just hitting the upload button. Crafting an engaging caption, using relevant hashtags, and strategically choosing where to share your video contribute to the overall success of your content. By following these steps and incorporating additional tips for optimization, you can increase the visibility of your Reel, attract a broader audience, and foster meaningful engagement with your followers. Keep in mind that Instagram's features may evolve, so staying updated with any changes is recommended to adapt your strategy accordingly.

13.Post Your Reel

Introduction

After crafting a captivating Reel, the next crucial step is to share it with your audience by posting it on Instagram. This guide will provide a detailed walkthrough of the posting process, including tapping the "Share" button, exploring visibility options, and implementing optimization tips. Understanding how to effectively post your Reel ensures that your content is well-received, engages your audience, and potentially reaches a wider community on the platform.

Step 1: Satisfy with Your Reel

Before initiating the posting process, ensure that you are satisfied with your Reel. Review the video, cover photo, caption, hashtags, and sharing preferences to confirm that everything aligns with your creative vision and objectives.

Step 2: Tap on the "Share" Button

Once you are ready to publish your Reel, tap on the "Share" button. This button is typically represented by a paper airplane icon and is located in the bottom right corner of the screen. Tapping this button initiates the sharing process and makes your Reel visible to your followers.

Step 3: Understand Visibility Options

Instagram provides different visibility options for sharing your Reel:

Share on Your Feed:

- Choosing to share on your feed means that your Reel will appear in your profile grid and the feeds of your followers.
- This option ensures that your existing audience sees your Reel.

Share on Explore Page:

- Opting to share on the Explore page allows your Reel to potentially reach a broader audience beyond your followers.
- Instagram's algorithm may recommend your Reel to users with similar interests or engagement patterns.

Share on Both (Feed and Explore):

- For maximum visibility, you can choose to share your Reel on both your feed and the Explore page.
- This option combines the benefits of reaching your existing audience and attracting new viewers.

Step 4: Confirm and Preview

After tapping the "Share" button, confirm your visibility preferences and preview how your Reel will appear to your followers. Ensure that the cover photo, caption, and hashtags display correctly. This step allows you to make any final adjustments before your Reel goes live.

Step 5: Monitor Engagement

Once your Reel is posted, monitor engagement and interactions from your audience. Respond to comments, engage with viewers, and track the performance of your video using Instagram Insights. This data provides valuable insights into reach, interactions, and overall impact.

Tips for Optimizing Reel Posting

Timing Matters:

- Consider the timing of your Reel post to maximize visibility.
- Post when your target audience is most active on the platform.

Consistent Aesthetic:

- Maintain a consistent aesthetic across your Reels to create a cohesive and visually appealing profile.

- Consistency contributes to brand identity and viewer engagement.

Engage with Comments:

- Actively engage with comments on your Reel to foster a sense of community.
- Responding to comments builds a connection with your audience.

Utilize Instagram Insights:

- Utilize Instagram Insights to analyze the performance of your Reel.
- Insights provide data on reach, interactions, and audience demographics.

Experiment with Captions:

- Experiment with different types of captions to see what resonates with your audience.
- Consider using emojis, questions, or calls-to-action to encourage engagement.

Share Behind-the-Scenes Content:

- Consider sharing behind-the-scenes content related to your Reel.
- This provides insight into your creative process and enhances viewer connection.

Cross-Promotion:

- Cross-promote your Reel on other social media platforms, blogs, or newsletters to drive additional traffic to your Instagram profile.

Monitor Trends:

- Stay informed about current trends on Instagram and consider incorporating them into your Reels.
- Trendy content has a higher likelihood of capturing attention.

Collaborate with Others:

- Explore collaboration opportunities with other Instagram users.
- Collaborative Reels can expand your reach to a new audience.

Encourage Sharing:

- Encourage viewers to share your Reel by creating shareable and relatable content.
- Sharing increases the visibility of your Reel among the followers of those who share it.

Conclusion

Posting your Instagram Reel is the culmination of your creative efforts, and understanding the process ensures that your content is well-presented and optimized for engagement. By tapping the "Share" button, selecting the appropriate visibility options, and implementing optimization tips, you can increase the impact of your Reel on Instagram. Regularly monitoring engagement, experimenting with different strategies, and staying informed about platform trends contribute to a successful and engaging presence on Instagram. Keep in mind that Instagram's features may evolve, so staying updated with any changes is recommended for adapting your strategy accordingly.

Embark on a journey of creativity and connection as you dive into the world of Instagram Reels! May your content shine with innovation, captivate hearts, and inspire joy. Wishing you a reel-y amazing experience filled with endless creativity and the sweet success of viral moments

Remember, Instagram's features are regularly updated, and new tools and options may have been introduced since my last update. It's always a good idea to check the official Instagram help center or app updates for the latest information.

Printed in Great Britain
by Amazon